HARDPRESS.NET
HOME OF HARD-TO-FIND BOOKS

A Gross Literary Fraud Exposed
by Joseph Emerson Worcester

Address:
HardPress
8345 NW 66TH ST #2561
MIAMI FL 33166-2626
USA
Email: info@hardpress.net

A

GROSS LITERARY FRAUD EXPOSED;

RELATING TO THE PUBLICATION OF

WORCESTER'S DICTIONARY

IN LONDON:

TOGETHER WITH

THREE APPENDIXES;

INCLUDING

THE ANSWER OF S. CONVERSE TO AN ATTACK ON HIM
BY MESSRS G. & C. MERRIAM.

BOSTON:
JENKS, HICKLING, AND SWAN.
1854.

CAMBRIDGE:
METCALF AND COMPANY, STEREOTYPERS AND PRINTERS.

Cambridge, September 30, 1853.

MESSRS. JENKS, HICKLING, & SWAN: —

GENTLEMEN, — The fact that an edition of my " Universal and Critical Dictionary of the English Language," with a *false title and a garbled and mutilated preface*, has been published in London, has recently come to my knowledge; and I have had some correspondence on the subject with Mr. Wilkins, of the late firm of Wilkins, Carter, & Co., the original publishers of the Dictionary. As you are now the publishers of it, I send this correspondence to you, together with a correction of some false statements relating to myself, which the publishers of Dr. Webster's Dictionary have made and circulated very widely, with a request that you will get these matters printed and put in circulation, in order that this literary fraud may be exposed. I am sorry to have occasion to make such a request; but it seems proper that something should be done; and it is my wish that such a course may be adopted as may tend to set matters right, as far as the case admits.

I do not wish any thing ever to be said or done, in order to promote the circulation of my literary publications, that is not in strict accordance with truth and propriety, or that can give reasonable offence to any one. The world is wide enough, and the demand for useful books sufficient, to give employment to all literary laborers, who make use of proper means for preparing books which will promote the improvement of society; and I see no good reason for hostile contention between those who make such books, or between those who sell them.

Respectfully yours,

J. E. WORCESTER.

933871

LITERARY FRAUD EXPOSED.

Cambridge, August 24, 1853.

JOHN H. WILKINS, ESQ.: —

DEAR SIR, — Not long since I saw, in an English journal, an advertisement of a Dictionary published in London, in the title of which my name was connected with that of Dr. Noah Webster, in a way that I did not understand, and could not account for; and in the Boston Daily Advertiser, of the 5th instant, there is a communication with the signature of G. & C. Merriam, the publishers of Webster's Dictionary, from which the following paragraphs are extracted: —

" Mr. Worcester having been employed by Dr. Webster or his family, to abridge the American Dictionary of the English Language, some years afterwards, and subsequently to Dr. Webster's death, in presenting to the public a Dictionary of his own, of the same size as the Abridgment prepared by him of Webster, says in his Preface, that he 'is not aware of having taken a single word, or the definition of a word' from Webster in the preparation of his work.

" Now mark this fact. An edition of Worcester's Dictionary has recently been published in London, and sought to be pushed there, in which the paragraph we have cited is carefully suppressed, and is advertised as ' Webster's Critical and Pronouncing Dictionary, &c., enlarged and revised by Worcester.' On the title-page Webster is

1 *

placed first, in large type, and Worcester follows in another line in smaller type; and the book is lettered on the
back: 'Webster's and Worcester's Dictionary'!"

Now this was new and surprising to me; for I did not
know that my Dictionary had been published in London.
Since seeing this statement, I have called three or four
times at your office in Boston to make inquiry of you
respecting the matter; but did not find you in till yesterday. I had, however, seen Mr. Rice, who was lately connected with you in business, and he told me that the
Dictionary had been published in London, and that he
believed you had a copy of the London edition. On
seeing you yesterday, you said that you had a copy, and
that you would send it to me. I have this morning received it; and I am astonished to find that the title is as
follows : —

"*A Universal, Critical, and Pronouncing Dictionary of
the English Language : including Scientific Terms, compiled from the materials of* NOAH WEBSTER, LL. D. *By*
JOSEPH E. WORCESTER. — *New Edition, to which are added
Walker's Key to the Pronunciation of Classical and
Scripture Proper Names, enlarged and improved; a Pronouncing Vocabulary of Modern Geographical Names;
and an English Grammar.* London: Henry G. Bohn,
4, 5, and 6 York Street, Covent Garden."

The true title of my Dictionary is as follows : —

"*A Universal and Critical Dictionary of the English
Language : to which are added Walker's Key to the
Pronunciation of Classical and Scripture Proper Names,
much enlarged and improved; and a Pronouncing Vocab-
ulary of Modern Geographical Names. By* JOSEPH E.
WORCESTER."

I find that the *Preface* is garbled and much altered;
and several omissions are made. One of the matters
omitted in it is the following statement, viz. : — "*With
respect to Webster's Dictionary, which the compiler several*

years since abridged, he is not aware of having taken a single word, or the definition of a word, from that work in the preparation of this."

I do not know that the truth of this statement has ever been explicitly denied, and I do know that it has never been disproved. You will see how inconsistent—how false and injurious—is the statement in the Title of the London edition,—"*compiled from the materials of Noah Webster*"! The person who remodelled the Title and Preface of the London edition, must have known that he was contradicting the statement which I made in my Preface; and the publishers of Webster's Dictionary are endeavoring to make use of this dishonest proceeding of the London publisher to my injury, and in such a manner as no honorable or honest men would do, if they knew the facts in the case.

I would now ask, what is to be done in this matter? You will not suppose that I ought to feel satisfied to have it remain uncontradicted; yet I am very averse to appear before the public in any controversy relating to a publication of my own. You are aware, as well as other persons who have been concerned in publishing works which I have prepared for the press, that my habit has been to leave my books to the management of the publishers, without defending them from any attack, or doing any thing to injure any works that may come in competition with them; nor do I wish ever to deviate from this course.

As I have no pecuniary interest in the London edition of the Dictionary, I think I am entitled to be protected from being injured by it in this manner; and as you have made the contract, if there has been one made, with the London publisher, I must call your attention to the subject; and I do so in full confidence that you will wish to have the matter set right, and have no wrong done to any one.

Truly yours,

J. E. WORCESTER.

Boston, August 31, 1853.

MR. WORCESTER: —

DEAR SIR, — Your favor of the 24th instant came duly to hand, but I have not had leisure until now to answer it.

Early in 1847, Mr. James Brown, of the firm of Little, Brown, & Co. of this city, was about to visit Europe; and we (Wilkins, Carter, & Co.) authorized him to negotiate for the publication of your Dictionary in England if he had opportunity, and particularly with Mr. Bohn, from whom we had received an application for the privilege. Subsequently Mr. Brown informed us of an offer he had received from Mr. Bohn, and furnished us with the letter from Mr. Bohn to him; to the proposals in which we acceded, and in October of that year shipped the plates to London.

I remember perfectly well that we felt some doubt in regard to the validity of a contract made on paper not bearing a stamp; but we supposed Mr. Bohn was an honorable man, and would not repudiate it.

After shipping the plates we heard nothing from Mr. Bohn until the next year, when we became somewhat impatient of the delay, and we wrote him urging him to go on in fulfilment of his agreement. We received an answer stating that he was sorry the plates had been sent. And we learned that he had become interested in the sale of Webster's Dictionary. Several letters passed between him and us, but we were unable to induce him to fulfil his agreement.

In the autumn of 1849, more than two years after the plates were sent, Mr. Carter went to Europe for his health, — intending to see Mr. Bohn and come to some arrangement with him. But his health did not allow of this. In the summer or autumn of 1850, Mr. Bohn wrote us asking our lowest terms to sell the plates, which I named, — never dreaming that any other use would be made of them than that of publishing your Dictionary under your name. He accepted my offer, and the transfer of the plates was effected.

On Mr. Carter's return from Italy, in the summer of 1851, he brought home a copy of his (Mr. Bohn's) barefaced publication. You can judge of our surprise, I might say amazement, at the audacity of this literary fraud. We felt very uncomfortable about it, but did not see that any thing could be done to remedy the evil. Mr. Carter was never afterwards able to attend to business, and the subject of this publication was never further considered between us.

You may well think it strange that I did not at the time call your attention to the subject of this literary imposition; but as I did not see any means of remedying the evil, and knowing that the condition of your eyes was such that you could make but little if any use of them, I did not feel in haste to trouble you with a knowledge of it. I have, however, never seen any notice of this spurious publication in this country, until you called my attention to one. Had any such notice met my eye, I should certainly have deemed it my duty to call your attention to the volume brought home by Mr. Carter.

Had I leisure to narrate the details of our business transaction with Mr. Bohn, I think it would appear to be, on his part, as commercially dishonorable, as this literary enterprise is fraudulent and disgraceful.

Your obedient servant,

JOHN H. WILKINS.

In my letter to Mr. Wilkins, I say, in relation to the statement that " I am not aware of having taken a single word, or the definition of a word, from Dr. Webster's Dictionary, in the preparation of mine," that " I do not know that the truth of this statement had ever been explicitly denied." But the title of the London edition states that my Dictionary was *" compiled from the materials of Noah Webster "*! — and the publishers of Webster's Dictionary seem to insinuate very strongly, in the paragraphs which I have quoted, as they have also done on other occasions, that the statement is not correct. But if there is a word or the definition of a word that was, in the preparation of my Dictionary, taken from that of Dr. Webster, I am ignorant of the fact. Having had some knowledge of Dr. Webster's readiness to complain of improper use being made of his work,* I resolved *that, in preparing my Dictionary, I would forego all the benefit which might be derived from the use of the materials found in his work, so that I might not give the least occasion for an accusation of the kind, and might be enabled to make the statement which I did make, and which I challenge any one to disprove.*

Having felt it incumbent on me to expose the dishonest proceedings of the London publisher, it may not be improper for me to notice some other false statements, designed to injure me, which the publishers of Webster's Dictionary have repeatedly made and widely circulated. As these statements have not been publicly contradicted, they have doubtless done me injury in the minds of many.

The quotation above made from their communication to the Boston Daily Advertiser begins thus : — " Mr. Worcester having been employed by Dr. Webster or his family to abridge the American Dictionary of the English Language " ; — and in their Advertising Pamphlet they say, " Mr. Worcester was employed by Dr. Webster or his family to prepare an Abridgment of the American Dictionary," — accompanying the statement with injurious reflections. As this statement has been so often made in a form designed to do me injury, and as it is doubtless true that many persons may have been made to believe that there was something wrong or dishonorable on my part, I think it proper that the public should have the means of knowing the facts in the case.

---

* See Appendix.

The statement that I " was employed by Dr. Webster or his family to abridge the American Dictionary," is void of truth. The gentleman who employed me was Sherman Converse, Esq., the original publisher of Dr. Webster's Dictionary. So far was the task from being one of my own seeking, that I declined two applications that were made to me to undertake it, and one reason was the fear that it would bring me into some difficulty or embarrassment in relation to the " Comprehensive Dictionary," which I was then preparing ; but the matter was urged upon me by Mr. Converse, after I had stated my objections. If any one shall say that I committed an error in judgment in finally consenting to make the abridgment, I shall certainly, on that point, not contend with him, for it has been to me a matter of much regret that I did so, as may readily be believed from what has taken place. But I am conscious of having acted in good faith in the matter, and of not having deserved ill treatment from Dr. Webster or his friends.

After seeing the publication above referred to in the Daily Advertiser, I sent a copy of it to Mr. Converse, (whom I had seen but once, I believe, for more than fifteen years,) accompanying it with a letter, in which I requested him to give a brief statement of the facts in the case ; and I received from him the following letter : —

Newburgh, N. Y., August 31, 1853.

Mr. Worcester : —

Dear Sir, — Having been absent from New York for several weeks, I have but just received your favor of the 12th instant, with a copy of the Boston Daily Advertiser accompanying it. I have read the article in the Advertiser, in which your name is coupled with that of the octavo abridgment of Mr. Webster's larger work. Authors are sometimes sensitive, but really I do not think you have much occasion for anxiety in regard to your reputation, either personal or literary. But since you ask me to say whether I "know of any thing wrong or dishonorable on your part in relation to that Abridgment," I answer, *Nothing whatever.*

The simple history of the whole matter is this. I had published Mr. Webster's great Dictionary, and presented it to the public. The labor had cost from two to three years of the best portion of my business life, without any adequate remuneration. For this I looked to an Abridgment, and such future editions of the larger work as the demand might authorize. But if I published an Abridgment, I wished to stereotype it, and, as a business man, I desired it to be made by an able hand, and with some variations, of minor importance, from the original. On conferring with Mr. Webster upon the subject, he stated two objections to my views. He felt that he had not the physical power left to perform the labor in a reasonable time, and that he could not preserve his literary consistency and be responsible for the variations which I desired. Yet, as I had published the great work after it had been declined, and that not very graciously, by all the principal booksellers on both sides of the Atlantic, he was willing that I should derive any remuneration I might anticipate from an octavo abridgment. With these views and feelings, he consented to commit the subject to the mutual discretion of Professor Goodrich and myself; setting a limit, however, beyond which variations should not be made; and that he might not incur the least responsibility for such variations as the abridgment might contain, I understood him to say, he should give the copyright to another.

As soon as Mr. Webster had made his decision, which was probably a sacrifice of feeling on his part to do me a favor, I applied to *you* to undertake the labor. You declined, and so decidedly that I made a visit to Cambridge for the sole purpose of urging your compliance with my request. You assured me that you could not undertake to abridge Mr. Webster's Dictionary, for the very good reason that you had then already made considerable progress in preparing a Dictionary of your own. At the same time, you showed me a Synopsis of words of disputed pronunciation, with the respective authorities. But the result of our interview was an agreement on your part to abridge the Dictionary for me, and to allow me to use your Synopsis, with the express reservation of the right to use it as your own, for your own Dictionary. And I must say that my persuasive powers were very severely taxed in securing the desired result.

I returned to New Haven, and subsequently called on you in company with Mr. Goodrich, when the matter of variations was settled, and you entered upon the labor; and I am free to say you performed it to my entire satisfaction, and I believe to that of Professor Goodrich also, for I never heard an intimation to the contrary.

I am very faithfully yours,
S. CONVERSE.

It may not perhaps be improper for me to give brief extracts from letters which I received from Dr. Webster and Professor Goodrich, very soon after they had been informed that I "had consented to undertake the abridgment."

The following is an extract from a letter of Dr. Webster to me, dated New Haven, July 27, 1828: —

" Sir, — Mr. Converse has engaged you to abridge my Dictionary, and has requested me to forward you the copy of the first volume. This was unexpected to me; but under the circumstances, I have consented to it, and shall send the copy."

The following is an extract from a letter of Professor Goodrich to me, dated Yale College, July 28, 1828: —

" My dear Sir, — Mr. Converse, who was here on Saturday, informed us that you had consented to undertake the abridgment of Mr. Webster's Dictionary. This gives me

2

and Mr. Webster's other friends the highest satisfaction; for there is no man in the United States, as you know from conversation with me, who would be equally acceptable."

The publishers of Webster's Dictionary, in order to make it appear that I have been inconsistent with myself in relation to *orthography*, say: " In 1827, an edition of Todd's Johnson's Dictionary, 1 vol. 8vo, was published in Boston, of which Mr. Worcester was the American editor. *Having the entire control of the matter*, he retained the *k* in words terminating in *c*, as *musick*, *physick*, *almanack*, &c., and the *u* in *honour*, *favour*, *authour*, and that large class of words." And they say further, in relation to orthography : " Worcester, not guided by any system or principles of his own, but seeking to fall in with the constantly changing practice of the hour," &c.

"Johnson's English Dictionary, as improved by Todd and abridged by Chalmers, with Walker's Pronouncing Dictionary combined," first published in Boston in 1827, was edited by me on principles fixed upon by the publishers and some literary gentlemen, who were their counsellors in the matter; and of these counsellors, the one who did the most in the business was the late learned and much respected Mr. John Pickering. It was made my duty to conform to the principles established for my guidance; and *I had no " control of the matter."* The Dictionary was to contain *Johnson's orthography*, and *Walker's pronunciation.* I was so far from defending the use of the final *k* in *music, physic,* &c., that I said in relation to it, in my Preface to that Dictionary : " The general usage, both in England and America, is at present so strongly in favor of its omission, that the retaining of it seems now to savor of affectation or singularity."

As the orthography of this Dictionary was that of Johnson, so the orthography of the Abridgment of Webster's Dictionary made by me, was that of Webster, with some variations which were decided upon by "his representative," and over which I had no control. The only orthography for which I am responsible is that found in my own Dictionaries.

These publishers further charge me with "adopting several of Dr. Webster's peculiarities, omitting the *k* and *u*," &c. I am not aware of having adopted any of Dr. Webster's "peculiarities" relating either to orthography or pronunciation; and if any such can be found in my Dictionary, I should certainly not regard them as adding to the value of the work.

With respect to the omission of *k* in *music, public, &c.,* it may be stated, in addition to what is said above, that it was omitted in that class of words in Martin's English Dictionary, published in 1749, before that of Johnson; and it has been omitted in many other Dictionaries published since; and the omission of *u* in *honor, favor,* &c. was countenanced in the Dictionaries of Ash and Entick, published long before that of Dr. Webster. The fact that this orthography was the prevailing usage with the best authors in this country was a good reason for adopting it.

There are other falsehoods relating to me, contained in the Advertising Pamphlet of these publishers, which I pass by without particular notice.

———

With respect to the manner in which my Dictionary has generally been noticed in Reviews and Literary Journals, so far as I have seen such notices, I have reason to be entirely satisfied. There is, however, an article upon it in the American Review, published in New York, (written, as I have been informed, by a Professor at New Haven, at the time when the new edition of Dr. Webster's Dictionary was preparing at that place, and who assisted the Editor in preparing that edition,) which is in remarkable contrast to any other review of the work that I have seen. The reputed author of this article has been employed by the publishers of Dr. Webster's Dictionary as a public advocate of that work; and his notice of mine is so much to their purpose, that they have seen fit to insert a great part of it in their Advertising Pamphlet. Considering the circumstances under which this article was written, and the manifest object of it, such of the alleged imperfections in the Dictionary as are founded in truth, are not greater or more numerous than might reasonably be expected.

As a specimen of the candor and truthfulness of the writer of this review, I quote a part of what he says in relation to what the author of the Dictionary has done with respect to words differently pronounced by different orthoëpists: — "He has," says the reviewer, "collected and attached to every important word, every method of pronouncing it that has ever been recommended by a writer, whether great or small, conceited or well-informed, judicious or affected."

Now the following is the true statement of what is done, in the Dictionary, in relation to words differently pronounced by different orthoëpists, as may be seen on page xxiv.: — "The English authorities most frequently cited in this volume are Sheridan, Walker, Perry, Jones, Enfield, Fulton and Knight, Jameson, Knowles, Smart, and Reid, all of whom are authors of Pronouncing Dictionaries. In addition to these, various other English lexicographers and orthoëpists are frequently brought forward, as Bailey, Johnson, Kenrick, Ash, Dyche, Barclay, Entick, Scott, Nares, Maunder, Crabb, and several others; besides the distinguished American lexicographer, Dr. Webster."

There has been, as I have understood, considerable controversy relating to the Dictionaries in the newspapers and literary journals, particularly in the city of New York; but it took place when I had little use of my eyesight, and I have seen little of it. While my Dictionary was passing through the press, one of my eyes became blind by a cataract, and not a great while after, the sight of the other eye was lost in the same way; and though my eyesight has been in some measure restored, yet for a great portion of the time since its failure, I have been able to do little or nothing as a student; so that it has been impossible for me to make such a revision of my different publications, as I might otherwise have done.

The manner in which my literary productions have generally been noticed by the press and patronized by the public, calls for the expression of gratitude much more than for complaint. It is with great reluctance that I have been induced to appear before the public in a manner that may savor so much of egotism; but the base conduct of the London publisher especially seemed to render it necessary that something should be done; and I trust that nothing which has here been said in my defence will be found inconsistent with truth or propriety. I have acted wholly on the defensive, and I have no disposition " to dip my pen in gall," or to make a hostile attack on any one, or to speak disparagingly of any publication that may come in competition with mine. I have not, so far as I know, ever seen or ever injured any one of the persons on whose course I have made strictures. Whether their consciences are at ease in this matter or not, is a question that concerns themselves more than it does me. For myself, I would rather be the subject than the perpetrator of such falsehood and wrong.

J. E. WORCESTER.

2*

APPENDIX.

As the question respecting the use made of " the materials of Dr. Webster " has become one of so much importance, I have thought, on further reflection, that it is proper the public should have the means of better understanding the reasons which induced me to take the course which I did, in preparing my " Universal and Critical Dictionary." My course, which was known to some of my literary friends, was objected to; for I was told that, by totally abstaining from such use of Dr. Webster's Dictionary, I deprived myself of advantages for improving my own, which I might, to some extent, without impropriety, avail myself of ; but I was sure, from what had already taken place, that I could not make such use, to a degree that would be of any benefit to me, without subjecting myself to such reproach as would be very unpleasant. I therefore merely cited Dr. Webster's authority in relation to words differently pronounced by different orthoëpists.

The necessity, in order to avoid reproach, of my taking the course I did in relation to the *Universal Dictionary*, must be sufficiently obvious to all who know what took place with respect to my previous work, entitled the *Comprehensive Dictionary*, which was first published in 1830. In November, 1834, there appeared in the " Worcester Palladium," (a newspaper published at Worcester, Mass.,) at the instigation, as I was informed, of an agent for Dr. Webster's Dictionaries, an attack upon me, in which the following language was used : — " *A gross plagiarism has been committed by Mr. J. E. Worcester on the literary property of Noah Webster, Esq. . . . . . Mr. Worcester, after having become acquainted with Mr. Webster's plan, immediately set about appropriating to his own benefit the valuable labors, acquisitions, and productions of Mr. Webster. . . . . . If we had a statute which could fix its grasp on those who pilfer the products of mind, as readily as our laws embrace the common thief, Mr. Worcester would hardly escape with a light mulct.*"

At this time the " Christian Register," published in Boston, was edited by Professor Sidney Willard, who happened to be as well acquainted with my lexicographical labors and the circumstances relating to them, as almost any gentleman in the community ; and he answered this (as he styled it) " ferocious assault," in such a manner as he thought proper, before I had any knowledge that such an assault had been made.   In order to sustain his accusation, the editor of the Palladium enumerated *twenty-one words*, which he said " are found in none of the English Dictionaries in common use, and were undoubtedly taken from Webster's."   I thought proper to send to the editor an answer to his attack.   In a succeeding number of the Palladium, there appeared a short letter to the editor from Dr. Webster, dated New Haven, December 11th, 1834, in which he said, " That he [Worcester] borrowed some words and definitions, I suppose to be proved by the fact that they are found in no British Dictionary ; at least in none that I have seen."   Subsequently there appeared, in the Palladium, a letter from Dr. Webster, addressed to me, dated January 25th, 1835.   This was followed by an answer from me, dated February 6th.   Two more letters from Dr. Webster followed, together with my answers.   The editor of the Christian Register transferred the whole correspondence into his paper.

By perusing all that appeared in these two newspapers, the Palladium and the Register, the reader would have the means of judging of the merits of the case, and would be able to understand something of the circumstances and reasons which induced me to take the course of abstaining entirely from the use of the materials found in Dr. Webster's Dictionary.   But as it might tax the patience of the reader too much to place before him all this matter (which may be seen by examining the files of those newspapers), I will now insert Dr. Webster's first letter to me, dated January 25, together with my answer.   This letter contains Dr. Webster's chief specifications against me, — a list of 121 words, " which," he said, "*primâ facie*, would seem to be taken from his Dictionary."   In his subsequent letters, he did not specify any more words as borrowed from him ; and the only word specified, with respect to which he accused me of "*adding his definitions*," was the word *clapboard ;* and in that, I may say, he succeeded no better in his evidence, than with respect to the charge of borrowing the 121 words.   The reader will please to compare the specifications and the evidence with the charges against me, quoted from the Worcester Palladium, and characterize the whole transaction as he may see fit.

MR. WEBSTER'S LETTER.

From the Worcester Palladium.

New Haven, January 25, 1835.

MR. J. E. WORCESTER : —

SIR, — Before I saw, in the Worcester Palladium, a charge against you of committing plagiarism on my Dictionary, I had not given much attention to your Dictionary. Nor have I now read and compared with mine one tenth part of the work. But in running over it, in a cursory manner, I have collected the following words, which, *primâ facie*, would seem to have been taken from my Dictionary : —

Abatable	Hydrant	Olivaceous
Assignor	Irredeemable	Ophiologist
Augean	Instanter	Ophiology
Bateau	Isothermal	Philosophism
Cartrut	Johannes	Phosphoresce
Caucus	Judiciary (*noun*)	Phosphorescence
Chowder	Kumiss	Phosphorescent
Congregationalist	Land-office	Prayerful
Congressional	Lapstone	Prayerless
Clapboard	Landslip	Promisee
Dell	Leach	Pappoose
Dutiable	Leachtub	Pistareen
Deliquesce	Magnetize	Pledgee
Digraph	Mazology	Postfix
Emphasize	Mishna	Postnote
Effloresce	Moccason	Raca
Educational	Monitorial	Ramadan
Effervescent	Muscovado	Razee
Electioneer	Muskrat, *or*	Redemptioner
Farrow	Musquash	Rhabdology
Fructescence	Notarial	Rock-crystal
Fracas	Neap (*of a cart,* &c.)	Roil, roily
Glazing	Neptunian	Repealable
Governmental	Outlay	Safety-valve
Grandjury	Obsidian	Semiannual
Graphite	Obstetrics	Sectional
Griddle	Ochlocracy	Sabianism

Saltrheum	Succotash	Tuffoon
Savings-bank	Selectman	Uranology
Scorify	Sparse	Varioloid
Scow	Sou	Vapor-bath
Sheepshead	Souvenir	Vermivorous
Spry	Suffix, *n. & v.*	Vishna
Squirm	Tirade	Voltaism
Spinning-jenny	Tenderloin	Volcanist
Spinning-wheel	Teraphim	Waffle
Seraskier	Test, *v.*	Whiffletree
Siderography	Thammuz	Wilt
Siderographical	Tetaug	Winter-kill
Slump	Tomato	Zumology.

I will thank you, Sir, to state in what other Dictionary, except mine, you found the foregoing words, and how many or which you borrowed from mine.

Your compliance with this request will oblige

Your humble servant,
N. Webster.

MR. WORCESTER'S ANSWER.

Cambridge, February 6, 1835.

Dr. Noah Webster: —

Sir, — On Friday last I received a copy of the Worcester Palladium, in which was found a letter addressed by you to me, containing a list of one hundred and twenty-one words from my Dictionary, "which," you say, "*primâ facie*, would seem to have been taken from your Dictionary"; and you add that you "will thank me to state in what other Dictionary, except yours, I found the words, and how many or which I borrowed from yours."

As a lawyer, Sir, you are aware, that, when an accusation is made, the burden of the proof lies not with the accused, but with the accuser. It might not, therefore, perhaps be improper for me to take the ground that your request is an unreasonable one, and for that reason to decline to comply with it. I will not, however, avail myself of this right. I think I may truly say that in my transactions with you, it has been my intention to act uprightly and faithfully, nor do I know that an individual of those who are most acquainted with the facts (yourself excepted) has a different impression. In answer to the charges which have appeared against me in the Worcester Palladium, I have already made some statements of facts, none of which, so far as I know, have been, or can be, disproved. You now call for something further, and it shall be cheerfully granted. I feel indeed gratified by the manner in which you have been pleased to make the request; for though I have no love of contention, yet if I must be dragged into a newspaper controversy in defence of myself in this matter, I should prefer that, of all men in the world, it should be with yourself, writing under your own name.

You evidently supposed, Sir, that none of the words in your list were to be found in any Dictionary that was published before the appearance of your work; but I confess I am somewhat surprised at this fact, inasmuch as, from your reputation as a lexicographer, it might naturally be supposed that you were extensively acquainted with works of this sort, and especially with the works which are so well known to all persons who have any just pretensions to much knowledge of this kind of literature, as are the several publications which I shall name. I shall not go out of my own library, or mention any work that I was not in the habit of consulting in preparing my Dictionary.

Of the *one hundred and twenty-one* words in your list, *eighteen* are found in an edition of Bailey's Dictionary, published more than a century ago, and *twenty-one* in a later edition; *thirty-five*, in Ash's Dictionary, published in 1775; *thirty-seven*, in Todd's Johnson's Dictionary combined with Walker's, edited by *J. E. Worcester*, and published before the appearance of yours; *twenty-one*, in Mr. Pickering's Vocabulary, published in 1816; not less than *thirty* in the Encyclopædia Americana, and nearly as many in Brewster's New Edinburgh Encyclopædia; — and in these several works, upwards of *ninety* of the words are found, and many of them several times repeated. I have, in addition to the works above mentioned, about fifty English Dictionaries and Glossaries, in a majority of which I have ascertained that more or less of the words in question are to be found, but I have not leisure, at present, to go through a minute examination of them.

Of your hundred and twenty-one words, *six* or *seven* are not to be found, so far as I can discover, in your Quarto Dictionary, and one of them is one of those *three thousand words* which are contained in Todd's Johnson's Dictionary, but are *not* to be found in your great work, and which were inserted by me in the octavo abridgment of your Dictionary. Whether any of the others are among the words which were inserted in the abridgment at my suggestion, I cannot say with certainty.

From the preceding statement, you may perceive, Sir, that your *primâ facie* evidence is sufficiently disposed of, as it respects the most of the words. in question. You inquire " in what other *Dictionary* " the words are to be found; and in your former communication to the Worcester Palladium, you were so candid as to say, " that I borrowed some words from you, you suppose to be *proved* by the fact that they are found in no British Dictionary; at least in none that you have seen." Now, Sir, it appears to me that it would be quite as sound logic to infer from the above statements, that you have not seen, or at least have not carefully examined, many British Dictionaries, as it would to infer, with respect to a list of words, that because you do not know of their existence in British Dictionaries, they must, therefore, have been taken from yours; for it appears sufficiently evident that there may be words in British Dictionaries that you are not aware of. You seem also to have overlooked the circumstance that there are, besides Dictionaries, other sources for obtaining words, which are open to me, as well as to you; and if my success in finding words *out of* Dictionaries should bear as good a comparison with yours, as it seems to bear in finding the words in question *in* them (I only put the case hypothetically), it would not appear very wonderful, if I were able to find the few remaining words without any assistance from your labors. Of the hundred and twenty-one words, you have given authorities, in your Dictionary, for only thirty-nine; but I can, without going out of my own library, furnish authorities, in all cases different from yours, for upwards of a hundred of them.

With respect to your inquiry, how many or which words I borrowed from you, I have already said that I did not know that a single one was inserted on your sole authority. I do not affirm this to have been the fact, for I am aware that oversights of this sort may happen; but if any have been so inserted, I sincerely regret the circumstance, and will engage to erase from my Dictionary every word that you will prove to have been thus inserted. But if I saw in your Dictionary a word with which I was familiar, or which I knew was in established use, or found in respectable authors, I regarded it as a word belonging, not exclusively to any individual, but to all who write and speak the language, to be used by them on all proper occasions, even though it was not to be found in any Dictionary but yours. Take, for example, the very common compound word *semi-annual*, one in your list, which is not to be found in any of the English Dictionaries that I have examined, and you are entitled to the merit, so far as I know, of having been the first to insert this word in a Dictionary; yet you cannot doubt that I was familiar with this word before your Dictionary was published; and as I have had occasion to use it repeatedly in my other publications, I thought myself authorized to insert it also in my Dictionary. All the words in your own Dictionary were surely to be found in Dictionaries previously published, or had been previously used by other persons, except such as you coined or stamped anew, in order to enrich or embellish the language; and with regard to all words which owed their origin or new form to you, such as *ammony, bridegoom, canail, ieland, naivty, nightmar, prosopopy,* &c., it has been my intention scrupulously to avoid them, as being your own property, and I have not even inserted them in my Vocabulary of Words of Various Orthography, being willing that you should for ever have the entire and exclusive possession and use of them. There is a considerable number of words in my Dictionary which are not to be found in yours; yet they have all, I believe, had the sanction of respectable usage : I can therefore claim no exclusive property in them; and you are perfectly welcome, as I have before intimated to you, to have them all inserted in your Dictionary.

Should you be disposed, Sir, to pursue the examination of my Dictionary further, and honor me with any more of your inquiries, I will attend to them as promptly as my engagements may render it convenient.

Having paid such attention to your request as my engagements have permitted, and answered your inquiry, in some measure, I trust, to your satisfaction, I would now, Sir, respectfully make a request of you, which is, *that you would be so good as to inform me whether the charges against me in the Worcester Palladium were occasioned by any statements made by you, or whether you have ever made, or are now ready to make, any such statements.*

Your compliance with this request will oblige

Your humble servant,

J. E. WORCESTER.

APPENDIX II.

WHEN the preceding pages were issued from the press, I hoped I should not have occasion to make any addition to them; but some circumstances have since occurred which seem to render it proper that I should add a second Appendix.

Soon after the pamphlet was printed, I sent a copy of it to the Rev. Prof. Chauncey A. Goodrich, D.D., Dr. Webster's son-in-law, who acted as his literary representative in relation to the Abridgment, and who was the editor of the last edition of Dr. Webster's Dictionary; and, accompanying the pamphlet, I wrote to Professor Goodrich a letter from which the following is an extract: —

"It is doubtless true that there are some things stated in the pamphlet that may be unpleasant to some persons; yet I hope there is nothing said that any one has good reason to complain of; if there is, I shall be glad to have it corrected. In our correspondence, long since, in relation to the Abridgment of Dr. Webster's Dictionary, you expressed great satisfaction with respect to my management of the matter; and you have never intimated to me that you thought I had done any thing wrong or improper, in relation to that work, at the time of performing the labor of abridging it, or since. I cannot doubt that you suppose I have been unjustly censured, and that I have little reason to fear the strictest scrutiny on the subject. I am not aware that my character has suffered in the estimation of those who know best the facts in the case; though doubtless many have been made to believe the false charges that have been made against me."

Professor Goodrich in a courteous letter (dated November 2d, 1853,) in answer to mine, said, —

"It is perfectly true, as you say, that I was entirely satisfied with respect to your management in abridging the American Dictionary. I have always spoken, in high terms, of the exactness and delicacy with which you conducted that difficult concern. *I have also always felt and said, that I knew of no ground whatever for any imputation upon you, as though you had made use of Dr. Webster's Dictionary in the production of your own. On the contrary, I have uniformly stated, that you had acted, in my view, with great delicacy on this subject; and that if any coincidences should be discovered between the two works, I had no belief they were intentional or conscious ones on your part.*"

In replying to Professor Goodrich's letter, (Nov. 21,) I said, —

"I am conscious of having intended to give no reason for any complaint, in relation to the use of Dr. Webster's Dictionary; but you must be aware that a very different representation has been widely circulated, and doubtless great numbers have been made to believe it to my injury. With respect to the Messrs. Merriam, I am surprised that you should say, in relation to what they have published respecting me, — 'If they have erred, I am for myself satisfied that they have done it through inadvertence, not by design.' It surely has all the appearance of 'design.' And I would take the liberty to ask you, if persons wholly unknown to you, should publish far and wide, things relating to yourself, equally false and injurious, whether you would not be likely to regard them as unscrupulous men of the world, and not as men who felt it incumbent on them 'to do unto others as they would that others should do unto them'?— and whether you would be likely to place them in the latter class, till they were ready to give as extensive a publicity to the reparation, as they had given to the wrong? If you will compare impartially all that they have published in reference to me and my Dictionary, with what my publishers have said, perhaps you may feel, that when they made the complaints [relating to my publishers] which you spoke of, you might with propriety, have referred them to Matt. vii. 5, for their consideration and benefit.

"I do not know but I have borne these false representations with as much patience as could be reasonably expected. I have not heard of any one's expressing the opinion that I have made more complaint than there is good reason for."

Early in December, I received from the Messrs. Merriam, a copy of a new pamphlet, in which, instead of making any reparation, they have added to the "falsehood and wrong," in attempting to defend what they have published; though I think I may safely say they have not disproved, and that they cannot disprove, a single statement that I have made in the preceding pages. I have therefore no occasion to modify any thing that I have said.

Soon after receiving this pamphlet, I wrote to Mr. Converse in relation to one of their false statements, as follows: —

"December 13, 1853. To MR. S. CONVERSE: — Dear Sir, I say in my pamphlet, 'The statement that I was employed by Dr. Webster or his family to abridge the American Dictionary is *void of truth*. This I supposed and still suppose to be strictly true. Is it, or is it not so? You were the only person that I had any thing to do with in undertaking to perform that labor, and I supposed you acted on your own responsibility, as in an affair of your own. The Messrs. Merriam, in their recent pamphlet, say, 'Our statement, we submit to you and the public, in its fair intent and spirit, is *not* void of truth, and you were employed by Dr. Webster or his family, through Mr. C., as their agent, to abridge his Dictionary.'

" Please to inform me, from your own knowledge of the facts, whether my statement is strictly true or not. Yours &c., J. E. Worcester."

Mr. Converse's Answer, dated December 19, 1853.

" To Mr. Worcester : — Dear Sir, You request me to say whether, in negotiating with you to abridge Mr. Webster's Quarto Dictionary, I acted as *agent* either of Dr. Webster or his family. My answer is that I acted as *agent of no man.* My arrangement with Mr. Webster and his family, was permission to make and publish an octavo abridgment of the large work with liberty to include some slight alterations from the original. The alterations were left to the mutual discretion of Professor Goodrich and myself, carefully restricted within a limit, dictated by Mr. Webster. This point settled, I determined to stereotype the work ; and as the whole responsibility of the undertaking rested on *me alone*, I could think of but *one man* to whom I felt willing to confide the important trust of making an abridgment which involved a risk so great. Your attainments and pursuits had eminently qualified you for the task, and I decided at once to engage your services if possible. Either before or directly after my correspondence with you upon the subject, I intimated my preference and purpose to Professor Goodrich, and received his cordial approval. The risk and expense both of abridging and stereotyping the Octavo Dictionary were exclusively my own. The family of Mr. Webster had no share in either, and I do not know that I ever disclosed to any member of it the terms of my contract, either with yourself or the type-founders. Yours &c., S. Converse."

In relation to the statement in question, which the Messrs. Merriam have repeatedly made in a way designed to do me injury, and which they still persist in, the reader will see that Mr. Converse fully sustains what I have said, that it is *void of truth.*

The Messrs. Merriam in their last pamphlet say, — " We take it for granted, that a person quoting, publishing, and circulating opinions and statements made by others, indorses those opinions and statements ; or else, disbelieving them, gives currency to what he knows to be falsehood " ; — and in their pamphlet dated May, 1853, they " publish and circulate " a letter which they say was " recently received from a distinguished teacher in Eastern Massachusetts." They do not give the *name* of the writer, or of the *place of his residence* (substituting blank lines, as given below) ; but according to their own statement, they " *indorse* " its contents.

The following short extract is a specimen of this letter.

" ———, *April* 13, 1853.

" Messrs. G. and C. Merriam : —

" Gentlemen, * * * * * About this time or soon after I heard of Worcester's Dictionary. The story came to me thus, viz. : — that Worcester was *at once a pupil and assistant of Webster*, and seeing that he, Webster, had taken a step in advance of the age, though not in advance of truth, and also that Walker was 'behind the time,' *treacherously* went to work, catering to the Walkerian taste of the day, and produced this '*bastard Dictionary*.' * * * * *

"Respectfully, and truly yours,

"――――――――――"

I will leave it with the reader to characterize such a course and such language as he may see fit ; — with the single remark, that, so far from having been " a pupil and assistant of Webster," I never saw him to speak with him more than three or four times during his life.

It is no part of my design to commend my own Dictionary, or to disparage any other ; — but my purpose has been to defend myself against the false charges which have been widely circulated throughout the country, with an intention to do me injury, and which great numbers, as I understand, have been made to believe.

A part of the correspondence between Dr. Webster and myself has been given in the preceding pages ; and I have been advised to bring forward the whole of it, which would probably not be desired by the friends of Dr. Webster ; and I might add other things relative to the subject ; but I wish to do nothing more than the case would seem to require. I would have it understood that I do not shrink from the strictest scrutiny in this matter. I will not now go into the inquiry whether, in the preparation of the last edition of Dr. Webster's Dictionary, an abstinence from the use of mine was observed equal to that which I practised in relation to Webster's. Greater liberty than I used may have been taken without causing any complaint from me.

As the matter now stands, I think I may boldly ask any one who has taken pains to understand the subject, whether in relation to Webster's Dictionary, from first to last, after all that has been said and done, there has been a single point of the slightest importance established against me ? — whether I have not been grossly injured by false representations without having given the least provocation ? — and whether there was ever known a grave charge to be made more completely destitute of support by evidence, or less creditable to those who made it ?

J. E. Worcester.

APPENDIX III.

IF the reader has perused the preceding pages, he has seen that it was made necessary for me to expose *a gross literary fraud* perpetrated by the publisher of my Dictionary in London; and that, in making this exposure, I took occasion to notice some misrepresentations and falsehoods relating to myself, which had been widely circulated in this country by the Messrs. G. & C. Merriam, the publishers of Dr. Webster's Dictionary, particularly in their Advertising Pamphlet, published in May, 1853.

As an attempt had been made to do me injury in relation to the fact of my having made, twenty-five years since, the Octavo Abridgment of Dr. Webster's Dictionary, it became important for me to obtain the testimony of Mr. Sherman Converse, the original publisher both of Dr. Webster's large Dictionary and of the Octavo Abridgment, — he being the only person who knew all the facts in the case. I had not seen Mr. Converse for a considerable number of years; when I last heard from him, I was informed that he was a "confirmed invalid"; I did not know where he then resided, or, indeed, whether he was still living; and I was for some time apprehensive that I should not be able to obtain any thing from him. But I was at length so fortunate as to receive from him the letter which is inserted in the preceding pages, beginning on the 11th page.

The first twenty-four pages of this Pamphlet were issued from the press in October, 1853. Soon afterwards the Messrs. Merriam published a second Pamphlet, containing an assertion relating to Mr. Converse, which furnished a reason for my writing to him again. I also had a Second Appendix of four additional pages printed in January, 1854, and in this Appendix Mr. Converse's second letter is to be found, on the 27th page. I also took the liberty to insert an extract from a letter of Professor Goodrich to myself (dated Nov. 2d, 1853), together with my answer. After the Second Appendix was issued, I sent a copy of it to Professor Goodrich, together with the following letter: —

Cambridge, Jan. 31, 1854.

DEAR SIR : —

I now send you a copy of a second Appendix to the small Pamphlet which you received some weeks since. I was sorry that I had occasion to prepare the Pamphlet, and I am sorry, also, that I have had occasion to add this second Appendix ; for I think I may truly say that I am a man of peace, and not disposed to contend with or injure any one ; but I suppose it is right for me to defend myself by stating the truth and exposing falsehood.

I have taken the liberty, as you will see, to insert extracts from letters that have recently passed between us, — which I hope will not, under the circumstances of the case, be thought an improper liberty. Whether you had read all that the Messrs. Merriam had published relating to me, when you wrote the letter dated Nov. 2d, I know not, and whether you will think proper further to defend them, you will of course judge for yourself ; but you must allow me to believe that, were you in my position, you would think no better of their conduct, nor bear it more patiently, than I do.

From information which I have recently received, I have learnt that the injury which I have sustained by the misrepresentations and falsehoods in relation to the use of Dr. Webster's Dictionary, which have been widely circulated throughout the country, has been very great, — much greater than I had heretofore been aware of.

It seems very unfortunate for me that I consented to perform the labor of making an abridgment of Dr. Webster's Dictionary. I undertook the task, as you are aware, with great reluctance ; yet there seems to have been no complaint from any quarter, that the work was not done in a faithful and satisfactory manner. The question relating to the use of Dr. Webster's Dictionary in preparing my Comprehensive Dictionary, was perhaps sufficiently discussed in the correspondence between Dr. Webster and myself ; the whole of which you will probably not suppose that I should be unwilling, as it respects myself, to have reproduced. With respect to the preparation of the Universal Dictionary, I do not believe that you can find, in literary history, a case of the kind, in which so scrupulous an abstinence from the use of the materials of a previous work (affording so valuable materials for the preparation of a new one), was observed, as was observed by me in relation to Dr. Webster's Dictionary. And I have the satisfaction to think that you, and all others who know most of the facts in the case, believe that I am well entitled to take the ground, and to have it conceded to me, *of entire exemption from all blame, from first to last, in relation to Dr. Webster's Dictionary ; that I have given no cause whatever for any complaint ; and consequently, that all the injury which I have sustained, or may hereafter sustain, in relation to this matter, has been, and will be, caused by the circulation of* MISREPRESENTATION AND FALSEHOOD. And is the circulation of these *misrepresentations* and *falsehoods* to be continued ? With respect to the *immorality* of so doing, it would seem that there can be but one opinion ; and it is equally obvious that justice demands, not only a discontinuance of the circulation, but also a retraction to be made and as widely circulated as the misrepresentations and falsehoods have been. And this, indeed, would give but a partial reparation of the injury done.

I write to you on this subject as to one peculiarly connected with and interested in Dr. Webster's Dictionary ; and I write, as you will perceive, with the feelings of one who is conscious of having acted, in relation to that work, with strict uprightness and fidelity, and who has been grossly injured without having given any provocation.

Respectfully and faithfully yours,

J. E. Worcester.

Rev. Chauncey A. Goodrich, D. D.

Soon after the second Appendix was issued, the Messrs. Merriam published a third Pamphlet, in which they inserted an extract from the above-mentioned letter of Professor Goodrich to me (dated Nov. 2d), of which, as they state, " Professor Goodrich, at their request, obliged them with a copy." In reference to this letter, and the use made of it, I thought proper to write to Professor Goodrich, as follows : —

Cambridge, April 14, 1854.

Dear Sir : —

I wrote a letter to you on the 31st of January, and sent with it a copy of " Appendix II." ; which I suppose you have received. In that Appendix I took the liberty to insert an extract from a letter which I received from you, dated Nov. 2d, 1853. By a Pamphlet since published by the Messrs. G. & C. Merriam, I perceive that you furnished them with a copy of this letter of yours to me, and that they have inserted in their Pamphlet an extract * from the letter in which you defend them from attributing to me a participation in the " gross literary fraud " relating to the publication of my Dictionary in London.

---

* The following is the extract from Professor Goodrich's letter to me, which is published by the Messrs Merriam on the 5th page of their third Pamphlet : —

" I saw him [Mr Charles Merriam] for a short time, early in August last, as I was passing through Springfield, and he then spoke to me of the London Title-page and Preface, which had been sent him by his brother, who is in Europe. He spoke of them in a way which showed that he had not the least suspicion of your being concerned in that transaction. He alluded to the discrepancy between your statement and the Title-page, only as showing the extent to which Mr. Bohn had felt himself to be driven ; since he was compelled to alter the Title-page and suppress your statement that you had made no use of Dr. Webster's labors. The whole tenor of his conversation showed me that he had no intention whatever to cast any personal reflections on you."

The Messrs. Merriam say, in this Pamphlet (p. 5), "Mr. Worcester should not have felt at liberty to charge us with attributing to him a participation in this gross literary fraud, when we had *not* so charged him." And after quoting the extract from your letter, they say, "We now respectfully ask Mr. Worcester, with these facts before him, whether it was just in him to reaffirm his injurious statements on this point." In answer to this, I may say that *I never so charged them, or thought of doing so, nor did I " reaffirm " any such thing;* and I was surprised at your undertaking to defend them from a charge which I never made, and which I did not then know that any person had understood me as having made. The supposition that I could have taken any part in that " literary fraud " seems too absurd to be believed by any intelligent person ; and how you or any one should suppose that I accused the Messrs. Merriam of charging it upon me, I know not. You will find nothing to countenance it in any thing that I have written. I said (pp. 9 and 10), " The publishers of Webster's Dictionary seem to insinuate very strongly, in the paragraphs which I have quoted (p. 5), as they have done on other occasions, that the statement is not correct," — namely, the statement, " that I am not aware of having taken a single word, or the definition of a word, from Dr. Webster's Dictionary." This is what I said in relation to this point, and what I understood, and what others have understood, them to insinuate. But of this you took no notice. In my second Appendix I say (p. 26), and I now repeat it, — " I think I may safely say that they [the Messrs. Merriam] have not disproved, and that they cannot disprove, a single statement that I have made."

I am conscious that it has been my purpose to state nothing that was not strictly true, nor to use language harsher than necessary to " call things by their right names." A simple statement of facts, as I believe, is all that I need for a complete vindication of my course throughout, in relation to Dr. Webster's Dictionary. It has been my purpose to do nothing in relation to that work which should be ground of reasonable complaint. I have taken no part in any controversy relating to it, nor have I ever written a line, nor, so far as I know, induced any other person to write a line against it ; nor is it my intention ever to do any thing of the kind.

The Messrs. Merriam say, in their third Pamphlet (p. 7), " We do not doubt that Dr. Worcester, with great delicacy, and in a manner highly honorable to himself, conscientiously abstained from the use of Dr. Webster's work." This, it would seem, virtually acquits me from one of the principal charges which have been very widely circulated to my injury ; and so far, very well. But afterwards (pp. 9 and 10) they say, " We might suggest that we take it a little unkindly, that, in quoting from a private conciliatory letter of Professor Goodrich, his remark, ' *If* they have erred, I am for myself satisfied they have done it through inadvertence, not by design,' — thus in some sort assuming a concession that we *had* erred, — Mr. W. did not also give the extract we have quoted, or others from the same letter, stating facts which, in Professor Goodrich's opinion, exonerated us, chiefly or wholly, from the imputation of having ' erred.' '' This relates to the " extract " * above referred to as inserted in their last Pamphlet; but neither in that nor in any part of your letter did you distinctly allude to any charge which I had actually made.

They say in reference to me (p. 12), " Should our explanations be satisfactory to him, we shall be rejoiced." I would not wish to be thought too difficult or unreasonable in such a case ; and I doubt not that I am as well satisfied as you would be in having so injurious misrepresentations and falsehoods widely circulated in relation to yourself, and not explicitly retracted, when you were conscious of having given no provocation.

Respectfully yours,

J. E. WORCESTER.

REV. CHAUNCEY A. GOODRICH, D. D.

In their third Pamphlet, the Messrs. Merriam (as the reader may see in the accompanying " ANSWER " of Mr. Converse, p. 3), have published a garbled form of Mr. Converse's second letter to me, with remarks upon him not of the most kindly character ; and they have attempted to prove, and claim to have proved, some of his statements to be false. Mr. Converse has felt himself so much injured, that he has deemed it necessary, in order to vindicate the truth of his statements, to be at the expense of publishing the following " ANSWER" to the attack thus made upon him ; and he has sent his Answer to me in manuscript, with a request that it may be " inserted in a third *Appendix* to my Pamphlet, or printed in a proper manner to be circulated separately." I am sorry to be under the necessity of pursuing this matter further ; but it seems reasonable that Mr. Converse should have an opportunity to defend himself from the aspersions cast upon him. When I wrote to him, I had no expectation that he would be injured in this manner. That a gentleman — so prostrated, as he is, by misfortune and long-continued chronic illness, yet compelled, by painful efforts, to obtain his daily bread — should be subjected to such vexation and expense for doing what he did (to use his own words) " simply from a sense of duty," is to me a matter of much regret ; and one would think it would cause " compunctious visitings " in other persons concerned.

---

* This " extract " is inserted at the bottom of the 31st page ; and it may be seen, with the remarks of the Messrs. Merriam upon it, on the 5th page of their Pamphlet ; and in their remarks, they do not distinctly allude to any charge which I had actually made.

The reader will see how fully Mr. Converse establishes the truth of what he had previously stated ; and that he has shown, in relation to the statement so often made by the Messrs. Merriam, that I "was employed by Dr. Webster or his family to abridge the American Dictionary," that it is *void of truth.* This statement in itself would be of little importance, except for the hostile use that has been often made of it.

As representations, falsely charging me with gross plagiarisms on Dr. Webster's Dictionary, have been widely circulated throughout the country, and many persons, as I have been informed, have been made to believe these false charges, very much to my injury, it is high time that the public should have correct information on the subject.

I again drop this controversy for the present, — I hope for ever. I have kept back matters which, perhaps, I may have occasion here-after to bring forward ; but I hope it will not be necessary. As the case now stands, I am bold to ask the impartial reader, What offence on my part has been proved, and what statement that I have made has been disproved ?

J. E. WORCESTER.

May, 1854.

POSTSCRIPT.

SINCE the preceding pages were issued, the Messrs. Merriam have published another *Pamphlet,* which Mr. Converse has seen fit to notice. — *See page* 11 *of his* " ANSWER."

That a gentleman of Mr. Converse's character and circumstances — a witness wholly uninterested, and the only individual who has a personal knowledge of all the facts to which he testifies — should receive such treatment, may "astonish" others, one would think, as well as himself.

I will not venture to characterize this new Pamphlet ; nor can I undertake to re-mark upon all the matters that are remarkable in it. But I will, at present, merely request every person who may take an interest in this controversy, to read all that has been published on both sides, and ask himself, what offence, on my part, has been proved ; — or what statement that I have made has been disproved ; — how I could have pursued my literary labors in a more inoffensive manner than I have done ; — and whether, in what I have written on this disagreeable affair, (for a per-sonal controversy is to me exceedingly disagreeable,) my object has not been, not to injure others, but merely to defend myself from *misrepresentation and falsehood.*

J. E. WORCESTER.

September, 1854.

MR. CONVERSE'S ANSWER

TO

AN ATTACK ON HIM BY MESSRS. C. & G. MERRIAM.

Camden, N. J., April, 1854.

MR. WORCESTER : —

I herewith send you an Answer to the attack on me by the Messrs. Merriam, in manuscript, longer than I could wish, and perhaps longer than you may think necessary. I wish to have it published at my own expense, and, if you are willing, in a third Appendix to your pamphlet, that it may be read in connection with what I have before written. It is my wish to have it printed as it is, notwithstanding it contains a letter from yourself to me and my answer, which have already appeared. The words which are underscored I wish to be *italicized*. If you do not see fit to have it inserted in a third Appendix, I wish to have it printed in a proper manner to be circulated separately. I fear its length may deter you from allowing it to appear in the connection desired, but I have felt it necessary to give, somewhat in detail, circumstances connected with the relations I sustained to Dr. Webster and his Dictionaries, that others may see why he should naturally have felt desirous of yielding, in some degree, to *my* views and wishes in regard to the Abridgment, although so directly in conflict with his own. But for greatly impaired health, and the necessity of almost constantly travelling from place to place, I should have sent you my reply at an earlier day.

Very faithfully yours,

S. CONVERSE.

MR. CONVERSE'S ANSWER.

April, 1854.

MR. WORCESTER:—

On the 12th of August last, you addressed me a letter requesting me to say whether I knew "of any thing *wrong* or *dishonorable* on your part," in relation to the agency you had in making the Abridgment of Webster's Octavo Dictionary. I replied, "*Nothing whatever*"; and gave a short statement of facts in relation to that work. On the 13th of December following, you addressed me another letter, a copy of which, together with a copy of my answer, I here insert.

THE LETTERS.

"December 13, 1853. To MR. S. CONVERSE:—Dear Sir, I say in my pamphlet, 'The statement that I was employed by Dr. Webster or his family to abridge the American Dictionary is *void of truth*.' This I supposed, and still suppose, to be strictly true. Is it, or is it not so? You were the only person that I had any thing to do with in undertaking to perform that labor, and I supposed you acted on your own responsibility, as in an affair of your own. The Messrs. Merriam, in their recent pamphlet, say, 'Our statement, we submit to you and the public, in its fair intent and spirit, is *not* void of truth, and you were employed by Dr. Webster or his family, through Mr. C., as their agent, to abridge his Dictionary.'

"Please to inform me, from your own knowledge of the facts, whether my statement is strictly true or not. Yours, &c., J. E. WORCESTER."

Mr. Converse's Answer, dated December 19, 1853.

"To MR. WORCESTER:—Dear Sir, You request me to say whether, in negotiating with you to abridge Mr. Webster's Quarto Dictionary, I acted as *agent* either of Dr. Webster or his family. My answer is, that I acted as *agent of no man*. My arrangement with Mr. Webster and his family, was for permission to make and publish an octavo abridgment of the large work, with liberty to include some slight alterations from the original. The alterations were left to the mutual discretion of Professor Goodrich and myself, carefully restricted within a limit dictated by Mr. Webster. This point settled, I determined to stereotype the work; and as the whole responsibility of the undertaking rested on *me alone*, I could think of but *one man* to whom I felt willing to confide the important trust of making an abridgment which involved a risk so great. Your attainments and pursuits had eminently qualified you for the task, and I decided at once to engage your services if possible. Either before or directly after my correspondence with you upon the subject, I intimated my preference and purpose to Professor Goodrich, and received his cordial approval. The risk and expense both of abridging and stereotyping the Octavo Dictionary were exclusively my own. The family of Mr. Webster had no share in either, and I do not know that I ever disclosed to any member of it the terms of my contract, either with yourself or the typefounders. Yours, &c., S. CONVERSE."

When replying to your letters, I was not aware that testifying to your integrity in matters of mutual concern, twenty-five years ago, could give offence to living man. Up to that time, I had been ignorant of the misunderstanding between yourself and the Messrs. Merriam; I had seen none of the various publications in the controversy; had no concern with its merits; cherished no unkind feelings toward those gentlemen; and replied to your letters simply from a sense of duty to one whose high standing and honorable intercourse had challenged my respect from our earliest acquaintance. It seems, however, from your letter above quoted, that one part of the controversy had been narrowed down to the truth or falsehood of the Messrs. Merriam's assertion, that "you were employed by Dr. Webster or his family, *through me*, as their *agent*, to abridge his Dictionary."

My answer declared that "*I acted as the agent of no man.*" At this the Messrs. Merriam have taken umbrage, and made on *me* a *rude* and *unprovoked attack;* a copy of which I here insert, that they may have the full benefit of it, in connection with what I am about to say.

THE ATTACK.

" Now, in the first place, it is preposterous to suppose Dr. Webster ever gave such an unqualified license to any person to go forward and make and publish an abridgment of this work, the labor of his life, independently of his own control, as Mr. Converse's letter implies. Every circumstance in the case disproves such a position. The extract published by Dr. Worcester himself of a letter to him from Dr. Webster, of July 27, 1828, in which he says, 'Under the circumstances I have consented to it [Dr. Worcester's abridging the work], and shall send the copy,' shows that his assent was necessary. Dr. Worcester, likewise, himself expressly disavows having had any control over the orthography, &c., which he says 'were decided upon by his [Dr. Webster's] representative [viz. one of his 'family,' Professor Goodrich], and over which I had no control.' Nor had Mr. Converse the slightest. Dr. Goodrich, in his Preface to the Revised Edition of Webster's 8vo., published in 1847, speaks of the original Abridgment as ' made under the author's direction' by Dr. Worcester.

" Now hear Mr. Sherman Converse, in his sufficiently egotistical letter : —

" '*I* acted as agent for no man. . . . . . *I* determined to stereotype the work. . . . . *I* could think of but one man to whom *I* felt willing to confide the important trust; *I* decided at once to engage your services. . . . . . *I* intimated my preference and purpose to Professor Goodrich. . . . . *The risk and expense both of abridging and stereotyping the Octavo Dictionary were exclusively my own.* . . . . . The family of Mr. Webster had no share in either, and *I* do not know that *I* ever disclosed,' &c.

" We have obtained from the Executors of Dr. Webster's Estate, a copy of the Contract made by Dr. W. with Mr. Converse, from which the following are extracts : — ' The said Webster, on his part, having the fullest confidence in the ability and judgment of JOSEPH E. WORCESTER, Esq., of Cambridge, Massachusetts, he doth *authorize* the said Converse to *commit* to said Worcester the work of abridging said Dictionary into an octavo volume as aforesaid, on the following principles.' ' The pronunciation, as marked and indicated by characters in said Dictionary, shall be retained, and such other words . . . . . shall have their pronunciation indicated . . . . . by the use of the above-mentioned characters, and such additional ones *as said Webster shall furnish and point out.*' ' Should said Worcester doubt at any time as to the pronunciation intended by said Webster, the words in question shall be *referred to said Webster* for his decision.' ' Any suggestions made by said Webster, as to alterations and improvements, shall be attended to.' ' And the said Webster doth hereby agree that the said Converse *may retain five hundred dollars*, from the first payments due said Webster on the proceeds of the said octavo edition, *as his the said Webster's share of a recompense to said Worcester for his services in abridging the Dictionary aforesaid.*'

" Thus much for Mr. Sherman Converse. It will be seen that the statement in his letter is in direct conflict with the express language of the contract ; while the whole spirit of his statement is not less positively contravened by the spirit and tenor of this precise legal instrument. We do not think we need waste time in comment. If Mr. Worcester thinks it a state of facts on which to raise a question of personal veracity, we are willing to submit the case without argument to the verdict of the public. If the case were his own, we think we could quote a passage from Matthew which he might properly commend to the other party, 'for their consideration and-benefit,' which should lead them to be more charitable. Yet we presume Dr. Worcester never saw this Converse contract, — his direct negotiations being made with Mr. C. We bring no charge of want of veracity in this matter against him. Must he not concede he has been hasty in advancing such a charge against others ? "

Fortunate, indeed, that, unlike the phenomena in nature, the Merriam thunder is without lightning, and " I still live."

A waggish fellow-student of mine, in college, assured his professor that he could give Scripture authority for the crime of suicide. " Judas went and hanged himself " ; " go thou and do likewise."

If, by adopting the same rule of quotation, the gentlemen think they have gained a victory over *me*, let them look to their *laurels ;* they will find them *no Evergreens*.

To a clear understanding of what I had said, strict justice required the publication of both my letters in full, in connection with their attack. But they have preferred to invest the subject with darkness, rather than light.

My first letter they have omitted entirely, and suppressed what was essential in the second. Their quotations from the contract may have been made by the same rule. I have not seen that instrument for more than twenty years, but am content to take the extracts as they have given them.

Would my limits permit, it would afford some satisfaction to give you, in this place, a history of the origin and progress of my connection with Dr. Webster and his Dictionaries ; and to show you why he had failed to procure the publication of the original work, either in this country, England, or France, previous to the application made to myself.

Dr. Webster returned from Europe, with his Manuscripts, greatly disheartened, if not in despair of their publication. In process of time, Professor Goodrich asked me if I would publish the Dictionary. My answer was, Yes, on certain conditions ; one of which was that I should have the right, on fair terms, to an octavo abridgment. My conditions were accepted by Dr. Webster ; a contract was executed, and as early as possible the work was put to press.

But owing to a movement by Dr. Webster in early life, having for its object, as has been said, to correct the anomalous character of English orthography, by spelling each word as pronounced,* such was the prejudice in the community against him, as a Lexicographer, and such the misapprehension concerning the

---

* Whether Dr. Webster ever actually made such a movement, with such design, I have no *personal* knowledge ; but in laboring to secure favor for the large Dictionary, I found that the charge and belief that he had done so had become almost universal, and to that fact alone I could attribute the deep-rooted prejudice and utter misapprehension throughout the country, in regard to the real character of his great work. He was said to have published a small volume, which I have never seen, in which he gave examples of the changes proposed. The late Professor Kingsley, of Yale College, I am quite sure, told me that he had seen a copy, and quoted some of the examples, one of which was *noshun,* for *notion.* To the *belief* of this statement, whether true or not, I doubt not the prejudice and misapprehension were justly attributable.

real character of his work, that, before my agents could succeed at all in obtaining subscribers, it became necessary for me to confer personally with a great number of the principal literary and influential men throughout the Union; and by means of extracts from the manuscripts, and verbal explanations, to *disabuse* their minds. My efforts were so successful, that by the countenance and patronage of most of the distinguished gentlemen whom I met, and by means of written recommendations of the Dictionary from several of them, I was enabled to secure sufficient patronage to defray the actual expenses of publication, but by no means to remunerate for time and labor.

Among the great number of gentlemen whom I met for the purpose, were Mr. Pickering, Judge Story, William Sullivan, and Mr. Everett, of Boston; Chancellor Kent, Dr. Francis, Professor Renwick, and David B. Ogden, of New York; Matthew Cary, Judge Hopkinson, Mr. Duponceau, Dr. Rush, and members generally of the celebrated Wistar Club, of Philadelphia; John Quincy Adams, Mr. Calhoun, Mr. Clay, Daniel Webster, Mr. Wirt, and members of Congress from all parts of the United States, at Washington. By the time, therefore, that the first volume was out of press, my intercourse with the influential part of the community at large had become so extensive as to enable me to form a tolerably correct estimate of what would be popular or unpopular in a new dictionary; and led me to a decision to put the Octavo Abridgment in progress at once, if Dr. Webster would consent to sundry alterations and variations from the original. He had agreed to give me the right of an Octavo Abridgment; but then, he was expected to make it himself, or procure it to be made at his own expense, and only in reasonable time, after the publication of the original work entire. This brings me to a passage in my intercourse with Dr. Webster, from the history of which I shall not lift the veil. He has gone to his rest, and no man was witness to our interviews. Were he here, he would answer for himself, and would confirm my statements.

Dr. Webster was a man of peculiar temperament; his general health had become greatly impaired; his physical powers were lamentably prostrated; and his nervous system had reached a degree of excitability exceedingly painful to himself. In addition to all this, he was keenly alive to whatever might compromit his integrity and character as an author. Many months must elapse before the printing of the second volume of the original could be completed; and all the proof-sheets must be revised and corrected by himself. He, therefore, *justly said* that he could sustain no additional labor, and that I had no claim on him, *then*, either to abridge the work himself or to employ another.

Under all these circumstances, I had come to him with a proposal, not only to assume new burthens, but to make an abridgment, with alterations and variations from the original, to which he said he *could not submit*. Dr. Webster did not mean to treat me *unkindly* or *unjustly*, but I had placed him in a painful dilemma, and I do not believe he would ever have made the concessions he did but for a desire to do me a favor, superadded to the kind offices of Professor Goodrich exerted in my behalf.

The result of the whole matter was, that he gave me permission to employ a suitable person, if I could find one, to make the abridgment. He also gave me

permission to introduce such modifications from the original as he had consented to in conversation, and within such limits as he should prescribe; and, in conclusion, he added with *emphatic feeling*, "I shall submit the modifications to the discretion of Professor Goodrich and yourself, and that I may not be responsible for them as *author*, I shall give the copyright to *another*," naming the person. This same feeling, in regard to the integrity of his authorship, he afterwards manifested in his Preface to the Octavo Abridgment, as follows: —

EXTRACT FROM THE PREFACE.

"As the author of the original work has intrusted the superintendence of the abridgment to another person, he is not to be considered as responsible for any of the modifications already alluded to."

Dr. Webster's permission made me free to act, but before I proceed further let me here join issue with the Messrs. Merriam.

They say, — "You were employed by Dr. Webster or his family, *through* Mr. Converse, as *their agent*, to abridge his Dictionary."

I say, — that "*I acted as the agent of no man.*"

We shall now see which assertion will stand, and whether the other statements in my letters were *true*.

Dr. Webster left me to myself; his permission was to employ a suitable person, but he suggested no name. My first application was to *you*. After writing twice to you on the subject, and receiving a negative answer to both applications, I visited you at your residence in Cambridge. You were prevailed on to undertake the labor; and for the first time apprised me of the existence of your Synopsis of Words differently pronounced by different Lexicographers; and of the fact that Todd's Walker's Johnson contained a great number of words which were not comprised in the large Dictionary which you had consented to abridge. The use of your Synopsis I eagerly secured, as the best available substitute for what had been denied me by Dr. Webster, *namely*, the insertion of Walker's pronunciation in the text. Our contract was accordingly made to include both the use of your Synopsis and the insertion of the extra words from Todd's Johnson, which, if I correctly remember, were found to exceed three thousand. Our contract bears date July 11, 1828.

Having returned to New Haven, I called on Dr. Webster; informed him that I had made a contract with *you* to abridge the Dictionary, and requested him to execute a written agreement, confirming what I had done, agreeable to his verbal permission, and securing to me both the right to abridge and publish. Accordingly, his Contract with me was duly executed, and bears date July 26, 1828; *fifteen days* after my contract with you had been executed in Cambridge! Great candor, certainly, in the Messrs. Merriam, to "*presume* that Dr. Worcester never saw this Converse Contract."

At the date of *yours* it would have been difficult to see that which had no existence. But why did you never see or hear of it afterwards? For the good reason that you had no *concern* with it. The subject-matter of the contract concerned only Dr. Webster and myself. My having employed you to abridge, and his having consented to the introduction of various modifications from the original at *my* discretion, made it necessary for Dr. Webster to prescribe to *me* the limits beyond which I should have no right to introduce a variation ; that, if I should claim any thing beyond those limits, I might be confronted with the Contract. But for this necessity, the Contract would have contained a simple agreement to print and publish. This very feature in it shows conclusively that you had been employed by *me*, and not by Dr. Webster; and that I was to share with Professor Goodrich the discretionary power over the modifications within the limits prescribed.

Within, we had discretion; beyond, not a particle. Dr. Webster's authority was, there, supreme; and had the work which I had employed you to do been simply to make an abridgment of the large Dictionary, nothing would have been necessary on the part of Dr. Webster but to put the copy into your hands and tell you to preserve the integrity of the original.

It was the permission given for discretionary modifications by a third *independent* party that rendered limitation necessary, and the delegation of Professor Goodrich, as Dr. Webster's representative, to see that there should be no transgression. It should be borne in mind that the modifications were not of Dr. Webster's seeking; that no man suggested, or, so far as I know, *desired*, their introduction, but myself; and that he only granted with painful reluctance what he would have been better pleased to withhold.

My discretion, touching the variations, was that of a business man. I wished for such changes as, in my judgment, would either increase the popularity of the work or protect it against injurious criticism. Professor Goodrich denied me nothing I claimed within the discretion allowed ; but so careful was he not to transgress, that you will remember, while we were at your house settling instructions for your guide, he denied me a certain modification, till he had made a special journey to New Haven to consult Dr. Webster.

But if Dr. Webster had made the abridgment himself, he would have made it for *me*, and not for another. When, therefore, he gave me permission to employ *you*, he only authorized me to do for myself what, from pressure of circumstances, he could not do *for* me. Hear him in his own letter to you the day after his Contract with me had been executed : —

"New Haven, July 27th, 1828.

" Sir, — Mr. Converse has engaged you to abridge my Dictionary, and has requested me to forward you the copy of the first volume. This was unexpected to me, but under the circumstances I have consented to it, and shall send the copy."

Strange language this, if he had employed you himself to abridge his Dictionary, *through me* as his *agent*. The Messrs. Merriam quoted part of this letter ; the whole would have defeated their purpose. Dr. Webster has expressed in it his own views of what he had done in his Contract the day before, *namely, consented* to my having engaged you to abridge his Dictionary. My request that he would forward you the copy, and his promise to comply, shows the engagement with you to abridge to have been *mine*, and not his. The absurd supposition that, being the *agent* of Dr. Webster, I could have employed you on my own account without disclosing my agency, I pass by ; and yet, had such been the fact, you would have been quite sure to hear from *him* on the subject in due time.

But let me put myself in immediate contrast with the Messrs. Merriam on a single point.

They say, — "It is preposterous to suppose Dr. Webster ever gave such unqualified license to any person to go forward and make and publish an abridgment of this work, the labor of his life, independently of his own *control*, as Mr. Converse's letter *implies.*"

In the same letter to which they refer, *I say,* — "My arrangement with Mr. Webster and his family was for *permission* to make and publish an octavo abridgment of the large work, with liberty to include some slight alterations from the original. The alterations were left to the mutual discretion of Professor Goodrich and myself, carefully *restricted* within a limit *dictated* by Mr. Webster."

The Messrs. Merriam have *suppressed* this whole passage in making their extracts from my letter, and then have the face to assert that it *implies* exactly the contrary of what it *declares!* The mere school-boy understands plain English better than to say that my letter *implies* no *control* over the abridgment on the part of Dr. Webster. Nor could the thick skull of a Hottentot so obscure the perception as not to comprehend the *necessity* of an author's consent and authority either to abridge or publish his work.

But the gentlemen rely on the *Contract* to prove me to have been the AGENT of Dr. Webster.

What says that Instrument?

"He (the said Webster) doth *authorize* the said Converse to *commit* to said Worcester the *work* of abridging said Dictionary into an octavo volume."

And is *this*, language which such a man as Dr. Webster would have used, had it been his purpose to constitute and appoint *me* his *true* and lawful *agent* and attorney, to employ you to abridge his Dictionary? I had already employed you *fifteen days* before, and that *without his knowledge,* and he now simply gives me authority to carry out what I had undertaken. To *authorize*, simply gives a right to *act*, but makes no appointment and constitutes no *agency.* To *commit*, is simply to put into the hands or power of another, or to *intrust.* As the Contract was a legal Instrument, Dr. Webster then gave me legal right, power, or authority, whichever you choose, to put into your hands or power, or to *intrust* to you, the *work* of making the abridgment. In other and simple language, he gave me *permission*, under the sanction of a sealed Instrument, to employ you to abridge his Dictionary. And this I had already done, on my own responsibility and at my own risk and expense. But the performance of this *work* or *labor* of making the abridgment on your part, had no connection with Dr. Webster's *authority* or *control* over the *matter* of the Dictionary as *author.* Nor could it impart to the abridgment the least authority of your own.

The Messrs. Merriam have assumed false premises, and been led to assert, and pertinaciously maintain, what is, *per se,* a *falsehood*, for want of clear perception of what constitutes an *abridgment.* Far be it from *me* to believe the gentlemen would wilfully or knowingly utter a falsehood ; though I could wish that, in their extracts from my letter, they had been *less careful* to suppress the truth.

To say that the abridgment was made under Dr. Webster's authority, control, or direction, as *author*, is simply to assert a *truism* in relation to what is *inseparable* from the very *idea* and *character* of an *abridgment*. Dr. Webster was *author* of the large Dictionary. That work, therefore, embodied his *authority* as a Lexicographer. As an English Lexicon, it represented his *authority*; but such authority was based solely on his *authorship*.

And what is an *abridgment?* A mere *epitome* or *compend* of an original or more extended work, and carries with it, *from* the original, the full character and authority of *authorship*; and that whether made by the author himself or by another hand. Disconnected from such authority, it is no longer an abridgment. To have cut into the large Dictionary right and left, and altered, garbled, suppressed, added, and omitted *ad libitum*, would not have been to abridge the work, but to make a new Dictionary out of materials more or less filched from Dr. Webster, but in no sense representing him or possessing his authority. Purely to *abridge* the large Dictionary would have been to make a simple *epitome* of it, changing in no respect whatever the character or features of the original. That man, therefore, who does not *perceive* that an abridgment, preserving the integrity of the original, is in its own nature *inseparable* from the authority of the author, must have the *os frontis* of an animal of *stolid celebrity*. Dr. Webster, therefore, could incur no risk in allowing *me* to employ whom I pleased, if competent, to abridge his Dictionary, and this he very well knew. The only trouble in the case, as it existed, resulted from the discretion given to a third party to dictate *modifications* from the original to a certain extent. Such modifications could not carry with them the authority of Dr. Webster; but the Abridgment at large was intended to do so, and hence Dr. W. was elaborate in his precautions to guard the original against modifications he had not conceded, and was careful to disclaim those which he *had*. Singular man Dr. Webster, to have employed me as his *agent* to do, or, which would have been the same thing, to have done himself, that of which he declared beforehand he would not take the responsibility; and on which, when done, he enstamped the seal of repudiation. Perhaps the Messrs. Merriam will explain how this could happen. They are *astute* in argument.

But the Messrs. Merriam have published the Dictionary for years, and ought to have learned by this time that to *authorize* a party to do an act is *one thing*, and to employ a party as *agent* to do the same act is *quite another*. They are authorized to publish the large work, but do they publish it as the *agents* of Dr. Webster's heirs? If so, they were constituted agents by terms very different from *authorize*.

They ought also to have learned that an *agency binds* the *principal* for all expenses incurred, or agreed to be incurred, and frees the *agent* from all liability to the party with whom he contracts, and also to the principal, if he adheres to instructions.

I commend the gentlemen to the study of the Dictionary, and beg to introduce to their acquaintance the words *Courtesy* and *Candor*.

Dr. Webster did *not* make me his *agent* to employ you to do the *work* of abridging his Dictionary, or for any other purpose, but took special care that I should not be so in fact, or be held to be so in *law*. He did not mean to assume the risk, responsibility, or expense of making the abridgment. He knew very well the precise meaning of terms, and he purposely made use of such as would preclude all idea of my having acted as his *agent*, and therefore protect him against any liability which might be incurred by my acts under such *pretence*. He did, it seems provide in the Contract for indemnity to me to the amount of five hundred dollars, should so much ever be derived as copyright from the success of the publication. But that subjected him to no risk, responsibility, or expense in the outset; and even this provision, in the lapse of twenty-five years, had escaped my memory; and the Messrs. Merriam are welcome to any relief this semblance of discrepancy may afford them.

As to their *tart* allusion to my *egotism*, it is painful to be made sensible of having offended true modesty; yet even in this case, it would not be difficult to polish and return a shaft, with an *aim* and an *arm*, that might make it felt.

They have raked from the dust and repose of bygone years, a private contract with which they had no concern; have violated the confidence of its seal, for which they can offer no justification; and, by misconstruction of its simple language, have assayed to sustain a bad cause by a worse argument.

They have invaded the sanctuary of private feeling, and dragged forth confidential transactions and personal misfortunes,* having no relevancy whatever to the matter in debate, and committed them to the wings of the wind in pamphlets and newspapers. And *wherefore?* Simply because I had testified to your integrity and honor in matters between us, in 1828, and stated that, in employing you to abridge his Dictionary, I did not act as the *agent* of Dr. Webster!

Time has been when an attack so wanton, affording provocation so just, would have drawn from my pen a rebuke more scathing than they could have desired me to administer.

But if such testimony, and such a statement on my part, could awaken feelings in *their breasts* which could only be appeased by a sacrificial offering so *unholy*, I forgive them. I do *more*.

Such an enemy in one's own bosom must be like the Arch Fiend in Paradise, administering sweets to the taste to create bitterness in the *soul*.

To the injury so wantonly inflicted, I am by no means insensible. Yet I am happy here to say, in all sincerity, that the man does not live toward whom I cherish an unkind feeling; and at the same time to assure the Messrs. Merriam that they have my best wishes that misfortunes may never overtake *them*. It has always given me sincere gratification to hear of their success. I hope it may continue, and give them the means of extensive usefulness. Yet no man's mountain stands so firmly that it may not be shaken; nor is it crowned with fruits and verdure so rich and beautiful that it may not be made desolate.

They are in possession of wealth which, but for misfortune, would have been mine. And rather than misrepresent and abuse me, it would better become them to send me a copy of the Dictionary, handsomely bound, accompanied by a check for a liberal amount on their bankers, with a kind note requesting my acceptance

---

* The paragraph in the attack to which allusion is here made I omitted to copy, as having nothing to do with the question pending; and I think the Messrs. Merriam themselves, in cooler moments, and under the influence of better feelings, will regret its insertion in their pamphlet.

of both, in acknowledgment of riches derived from the large Dictionary, for which, *primarily*, they have been so greatly indebted to *my efforts* and *misfortunes*. They can well afford to be *kind;* I ask them only to be *just;* and now, either to frankly confess, through their pamphlets and newspapers, that they have misapprehended and done me wrong, or publish and circulate this, my third letter to you, as widely as they have circulated their unjustifiable attack on *me*. The public will then be in a position to render an intelligent verdict between us.

Respectfully yours,

S. CONVERSE.

Mr. Converse's Notice of what is said by Messrs. G. & C. Merriam, in Relation to the preceding " Answer."

Schroon Lake, N. Y., August 30, 1854.

MR. WORCESTER :—

Since the publication of my answer to the attack made on me by Messrs. G. & C. Merriam, my attention has been called to a new pamphlet of theirs. Whether you will think proper to notice it, I cannot say. If you should, I will thank you to insert this letter.

The Messrs. Merriam, I am told, are professors of the Christian Faith. When, therefore, they had read my answer to their attack, and seen that I had given them the full benefit of their attack in connection with my answer, I had a right to expect from them a frank acknowledgment, that they had misapprehended, and done me wrong, or a prompt publication and circulation of my answer in full, coëxtensively with the circulation of their own pamphlets. But surprised as I was at the garbling and misrepresentation contained in their attack, I confess myself now more than astonished. In looking at the portion of their pamphlet professedly devoted to me, the question was irresistibly forced upon me, " Can these gentlemen be really of sane mind ? "

As Christian professors, it is just to presume that they each have a *Closet*, which they do not neglect. In the secret communion of that secret and sacred retreat, let me request them in all kindness, to make up an answer for themselves to the following questions : —

First. — Was it consistent with truth, justice, or honor, òr with the precept in the Golden Rule, to represent *me* in their pamphlet as having made an attack on Dr. Webster, his Dictionaries, or his Publishers ? I have made no attack on either, and have only been compelled to defend myself against their own rude and unprovoked attack on *me*, at an expense I am poorly able to bear.

Secondly. — Was it consistent with truth, justice, or honor, to represent *me* as having thrown out " dark insinuations about Dr. Webster, which I hope not to be constrained to divulge"? I have made no insinuations " about Dr. Webster " or any other man. I said in my answer to their attack, " This brings me to a passage in my intercourse with Dr. Webster, from the history of which I shall not lift the veil. He has gone to his rest, and no man was witness to our interviews. Were he here, he would answer for himself and would confirm my statements." Also, that " Dr. Webster did not mean to treat me unkindly or unjustly," and that " I did not believe he would have made the concessions he did but for a desire to do me a *favor*," &c. And here the gentlemen say are "dark insinuations," which I have expressed the hope, that "I shall not be constrained to divulge"! I only ask the gentlemen to review this extraordinary passage in their pamphlet, in an honest hour, in that secret place where the heart is naked to the eye of Him who searcheth it. No misunderstanding or unkind feeling occurred or existed at those interviews, but there are grave reasons, not personal to Dr. Webster or myself, for not lifting the veil from their whole history. Were Dr. Webster living, it would give him pleasure to confirm my statements and to testify to the world that I am quite as well acquainted with all transactions between him and myself in 1828, as the Messrs. Merriam can pretend to be; although, with distinguished modesty, they have undertaken at this late day to instruct me and the public in the matter.

Thirdly. — Was it consistent with truth, justice, or honor, to wholly pervert what I have said in my three letters addressed to you, by such garbling and comments as to entirely misrepresent their plain intent and meaning?

Fourthly. — Is it consistent with truth, justice, or honor, to send out their garbled statements and misrepresentations, and refuse to circulate in connection therewith my answer to their attack on *me*? That answer contains all I wish to say, in reply to anything they have said or can say, having the least relevancy to the point in debate, which is therein clearly and fairly stated, although in their last pamphlet they seem to have quite forgotten it. I will now test their willingness to let the truth appear to their readers. I propose to supply them, free of expense to themselves, with such number of copies of my answer to their attack on me, as will enable them to send a copy to each individual to whom they have sent the attack, and if they wish it, I will pay them a fair price for the trouble of doing them up, and the postage on such as are sent by mail. Or if they will give me a list of the names of those to whom they have sent their attack, I will save them all further trouble in the matter. If they will assure me that they will so circulate my answer, and will state the number of copies required, they shall be supplied.

Fifthly. — Was it consistent with justice or truth, to undertake to make *me* a party to their controversy with *you*, when I had no connection with it, or interest in it, whatever?

The gentlemen seem willing to give me a hundred dollars to confess myself in error in this dispute. I doubt not they would give twice the amount, to feel an honest conviction that they had done me no wrong, and were not wholly in the wrong themselves. They have repeatedly complained of my having testified to *their injury!* Is it not marvellous, that testifying to your integrity and honor, in matters between us in 1828, should work such terrible injury to the Messrs. Merriam in 1854! Were they as truly *martyrs* as their zeal to be thought so is apparent, the history of John Rogers would be totally eclipsed by a simple narrative of their sufferings. But enough. It is not my purpose to make a reply to their very extraordinary misrepresentations in their late pamphlet, and my health is so prostrated, that writing is a painful effort. I only wish the gentlemen to review what they have said, and settle the questions I have proposed, in the manner suggested, and to circulate my answer to their attack as requested.

Very faithfully yours,

S. CONVERSE.

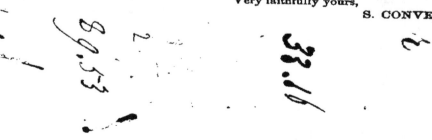